GRAYBEARD
★ LECTURES ★

Game Theory :
Because the Market Doesn't Sit Still

from the Whiteboard of
Mark "Dr. Maddog" Donnelly, PhD.

RPSS PUBLISHING – BUFFALO, NEW YORK

drmaddog@hotmail.com

The Graybeard Lectures - Game Theory: Because Markets Don't Sit Still

Perfect Bound ISBN: 978-1-956688-68-9

Printed in the United States of America

10 9 8 7 6 5 4 3 2 1

RPSS Publishing - Buffalo, New York

This book is dedicated to anyone who
ever left a meeting thinking,
We should have seen that coming.

The cap is off.
Let's play the game you're already in

TABLE OF CONTENTS

Introduction

Alright, picture this.

I walk into the room carrying a marker that's seen more boardrooms than most consultants, and I turn to the whiteboard. Not a slide deck. Not a clicker. Just a whiteboard that squeaks like it's clearing its throat before telling the truth.

"Today," I say, "we're doing game theory."

Half the room tightens up.

Someone hears math.

Someone else hears economics.

A third person quietly wonders if they missed a prerequisite involving Greek letters and regret.

Relax. If we were doing math-heavy game theory, I'd have warned you to bring a helmet and a calculator. What we're doing today is human game theory. The kind you've been playing since your first sibling negotiation over the last cookie.

Here's the dirty secret nobody tells you up front:

You already know game theory.

You've just never called it that.

Every time you've priced a product while wondering what the competitor would do.

Every time you delayed a launch because "let's see what happens."

Every time you ran a promotion that trained customers to wait for the next promotion.

That wasn't instinct. That was strategy. Sometimes good. Sometimes… educational.

So let's start by clearing something up before this marker runs dry.

Game theory is not about games.

There are no joysticks. No dice. No winners holding trophies while losers flip tables. Game theory is simply the study of what happens when your success depends on someone else making a decision while thinking about you making a decision about them.

Which means marketing is soaked in it.

You don't control the customer.

You don't control the competition.

You don't even fully control your own sales team once incentives get involved.

What you do control is how you think about the situation.

Now, here's where the whiteboard earns its keep.

I draw two stick figures.

One is labeled **"Us."**

The other is labeled **"Them."**

That's it. That's the whole setup.

If your strategy assumes "Them" won't notice you, won't react, won't adapt, or won't remember what you did last quarter, congratulations. You're not doing strategy. You're daydreaming with a budget.

Game theory starts the moment you accept a humbling truth:

Other people are not props in your plan.

They're thinking.

They're guessing.

They're misinterpreting your moves with breathtaking confidence.

And they're acting anyway.

Now, somewhere around this point, someone always asks the same question:

"So… are people rational?"

Great question. Short answer: yes.

Long answer: not in the way you hope.

In game theory, "rational" doesn't mean smart. It means consistent. It means people generally respond to incentives, habits, fears, and payoffs in ways that make sense to them, even when it makes your spreadsheet cry.

Which explains:

- Why customers punish brands for changing prices "too often"
- Why competitors copy the wrong thing and ignore the right thing
- Why "best practices" quietly herd entire industries into mediocrity

This is where the graybeard part kicks in.

After enough years, you stop believing strategy is about brilliance.

It's about seeing one move further than the room.

Not five moves. Not chess-grandmaster territory.

Just one move further than "we like this idea."

So during this lecture, we're going to do three things:

1. **We're going to name the games you're already playing.**

2. **We're going to look at why some of them keep ending badly.**

3. **And we're going to practice thinking just far enough ahead to avoid the obvious traps.**

No formulas.

No equilibrium proofs.

Just logic, incentives, and a whiteboard that tells the truth whether it's flattering or not.

Because the real danger in marketing isn't ignorance.

It's forgetting that the other side gets a turn.

Alright. Marker's uncapped.

Let's play the game you're already in.

This Looked Like a Good Idea at the Time

The whiteboard was already dirty when I walked in.

Not from today. From yesterday. And probably from three years ago. Ghosts of half-erased frameworks hovered like bad ideas that refuse to die. Someone had tried to clean it with a paper towel, which only spread the shame around evenly.

Perfect.

I pulled a marker from my pocket. It squeaked when I tested it. Good sign. A marker that squeaks has opinions.

"This," I said, tapping the board, "is not a lecture about game theory."

Everyone relaxed for half a second.

"This is a lecture about why your best ideas keep losing to other people's okay ones."

Tension returned. That was more familiar.

Here's the thing you learn after enough years watching smart people make the same mistakes with better fonts.

Most strategy doesn't fail because it's wrong.

It fails because it assumes nobody will respond.

We launch as if competitors are asleep.

We price as if customers won't talk to each other.

We reposition as if the market won't remember what we said last year.

Then we stand around shocked when the world reacts.

Game theory exists because someone finally wrote down the obvious and gave it a name:

Other people get a vote.

That's it. That's the whole scandal.

You don't need a PhD to understand it. You need humility and a longer memory than last quarter.

I've watched brands spend millions perfecting a move without spending ten minutes asking, "What happens when everyone else notices?" I've seen campaigns celebrated internally that trained customers to wait, competitors to copy, and sales teams to discount harder.

All perfectly rational. Just not well thought through.

Which is why we're not starting with equations.

We're starting with the whiteboard.

Because the whiteboard doesn't let you hide. It forces ideas out into the open where they can be questioned, erased, rewritten, and occasionally executed for cause.

Slide decks seduce.

Whiteboards interrogate.

And interrogation is what strategy actually needs.

Game theory, at its core, is not about predicting the future. It's about recognizing patterns in human behavior that repeat with depressing consistency once incentives, fear, pride, and limited attention enter the room.

People respond to signals.

They remember slights.

They punish inconsistency.

They cooperate when it makes sense and defect when it doesn't.

None of this is new. What's new is how often we forget it.

So this book is not here to make you smarter. You're already smart enough. It's here to make you harder to surprise.

We'll talk about competitors who react.

Customers who learn.

Markets that drift into sameness.

And why "best practice" is often just equilibrium with a nicer haircut.

We'll do it without math, without jargon, and without pretending humans behave the way textbooks wish they would.

Just a whiteboard.

A squeaky marker.

And a simple rule we'll keep coming back to until it sticks:

If your strategy doesn't account for other people thinking about you, it's not strategy. It's a wish.

Alright.

Let's clean a corner of this board and start where all good strategy starts.

With the uncomfortable parts.

Chapter One

You're Not Competing Against the Market. You're Competing Against Other People.

The first lie strategy tells us is subtle.

It doesn't shout. It nods politely and hands you a spreadsheet.

The lie goes like this: "If we just understand the market well enough, we can optimize our way to success."

Markets love that lie. Consultants adore it. Software platforms have built entire dashboards around it. The problem is that markets don't behave like weather systems. They behave like poker tables.

The market doesn't "do" anything.

People do.

Customers decide.

Competitors react.

Distributors hedge.

Sales teams reinterpret incentives like amateur lawyers.

And all of them are watching you while you're watching them.

That's where game theory begins. Not with numbers, but with awareness.

The Day Optimization Failed

I once sat in a conference room where a team had done everything right.

Research was impeccable.

Positioning was clear.

Pricing had been modeled six ways to Sunday.

The launch plan was laminated, metaphorically and emotionally.

They optimized every variable they could see.

What they didn't optimize for was curiosity.

Within weeks, competitors copied the visible parts, undercut the price by a hair, and framed the category in a way that made our "differentiation" look like table stakes. Customers didn't reject the product. They simply waited. Sales slowed. Panic meetings followed.

Someone eventually asked, "How could they do this so fast?"

Simple.

They were paying attention.

Game theory has a name for this moment.

Marketers usually call it "unfair."

Why "The Market" Is a Convenient Fiction

When we say "the market decided," what we really mean is:

A bunch of humans made choices based on limited information

while guessing what other humans would do next.

Calling it "the market" makes it sound neutral and external. Like gravity. Like rain.

But gravity doesn't change its mind when you launch a campaign.

Competitors do.

Game theory refuses to let you hide behind the abstraction. It drags the uncomfortable truth into the light:

Your move changes their move, which changes your outcome.

That's not economics. That's social behavior with invoices.

Strategy Is What Happens After Someone Notices You

Here's a quiet test for whether something is strategy or just planning:

Ask, "What happens when someone responds?"

If the answer is:

- "They won't"
- "They can't"

- "They shouldn't"
- *(or my personal favorite)*, "That wouldn't be rational"

You're not doing strategy. You're doing hopeful choreography.

Game theory assumes something deeply inconvenient:

Other players are not passive.

They are adaptive.

And they often respond in ways that make sense to them, not to your deck.

That's why pricing wars start.

That's why features converge.

That's why differentiation erodes faster than expected.

Not because people are irrational, but because they're strategic.

Rational Doesn't Mean What You Think It Means

Let's clear up a dangerous misunderstanding early.

In game theory, "rational" does not mean smart, informed, or correct.

It means internally consistent.

People pursue what they believe benefits them, given what they believe about the situation, even when those beliefs are wrong, outdated, or copied from someone else's PowerPoint.

Which explains:

- Why customers chase discounts and then complain about quality
- Why brands copy competitors and then wonder why nothing stands out
- Why organizations reward behavior they publicly claim to hate

Everyone is responding rationally to incentives. The incentives are just poorly designed.

Game theory doesn't judge this. It models it.

Marketing departments, on the other hand, tend to be shocked by it every budget cycle.

The Whiteboard Moment

This is where the whiteboard comes in.

I draw two boxes.

One says "**Us.**"

The other says "**Them.**"

That's it.

No personas. No quadrants. No arrows yet.

Then I ask the question strategy lives or dies on:

"What happens when they notice?"

Not hypothetically. Specifically.

- If we lower price, what do they do?
- If we reposition, how do they reframe?
- If we stay silent, who fills the gap?
- If we train customers to expect discounts, what do they learn?

Silence in the room usually follows. Not because people don't know the answers, but because they know the answers aren't flattering.

The whiteboard doesn't care.

The First Graybeard Rule of Strategy

Here it is. Write it down. Tape it to your monitor.

You are not competing against a static environment.

You are competing against thinking opponents with memory.

Once you accept that, a few things change immediately:

- You stop overvaluing clever moves
- You start respecting second-order effects
- You realize most "surprises" were actually predictable

Game theory doesn't promise you'll win.

It promises you'll stop being confused by why you lost.

And that, in marketing and strategy, is already a competitive advantage.

Now that we've admitted other people exist, we can move on to the next uncomfortable truth:

They don't just act.

They believe.

And what they believe about you matters more than what you meant.

Marker back to the board.

After the break let's talk about beliefs.

CHAPTER TWO

Rational Doesn't Mean Smart
(It Means Predictable)

There is a moment in every strategy meeting when someone says, usually with confidence and a laser pointer:

"They wouldn't do that."

That sentence has ended more marketing careers than bad logos ever could.

Because in game theory, that is not a useful objection. It's a wish dressed up as logic.

Game theory does not assume people are brilliant.

It assumes they are consistent.

And that distinction explains almost everything that surprises us in markets.

The Most Dangerous Word in Marketing

The most dangerous word in strategy is not disruption.

It's not innovation.

It's not even synergy.

It's **should**.

Customers should understand our value.

Competitors should realize that price war hurts everyone.

Sales should stop discounting at the end of the quarter.

The market should reward quality.

Should is the sound of incentives being ignored.

Game theory doesn't care what people should do. It cares what they will do, given the payoffs they see and the information they have.

Which is why rational behavior often looks foolish from the outside and painfully obvious in hindsight.

Rational, Explained Without Ruining Lunch

In game theory, a rational actor:

- Has goals
- Forms beliefs about the situation
- Chooses actions that seem best given those beliefs

That's it. No IQ test. No moral component. No requirement that the beliefs be correct.

If a customer believes discounts mean smart shopping, waiting becomes rational.

If a competitor believes speed beats elegance, copying becomes rational.

If a sales team believes their bonus depends on this quarter, long-term damage becomes rational.

From inside the system, everyone is behaving sensibly.

From outside, it looks like chaos.

Why Smart People Do Predictable Things

Here's the uncomfortable part for marketers and strategists.

The smarter the organization, the more predictable it often becomes.

Why?

Because smart people:

- Share the same data
- Read the same case studies
- Attend the same conferences
- Learn the same "best practices"

Which means they start thinking alike.

Game theory has a name for this outcome. Marketers usually call it "category norms."

Once everyone believes the same things about what works, deviation feels risky. Conformity becomes rational. Differentiation becomes dangerous.

That's how entire industries drift into sameness while congratulating themselves for being disciplined.

Predictability Is Not the Enemy. Unexamined Predictability Is.

Predictability isn't bad. In fact, it's often useful.

Customers rely on it.

Partners depend on it.

Trust is built on it.

The problem is when you don't realize how predictable you've become.

Game theory asks a brutal but necessary question:

If you were your competitor, what would you expect you to do next?

If the answer is "exactly what we're planning," you don't have a strategy. You have a schedule.

And schedules are easy to exploit.

The Whiteboard Test *(Again)*

Back to the whiteboard.

I draw a simple line:

Beliefs → Actions → Outcomes

Then I circle Beliefs.

Most marketing debates start in the middle or at the end.

- "The campaign didn't work."
- "Customers didn't respond."
- "Competitors undercut us."

Game theory drags the conversation backward.

What did they believe?

- About us?

- About the category?

- About their alternatives?

- About the consequences of acting or waiting?

Beliefs don't need to be accurate to be powerful. They just need to be widely shared.

That's why perception beats intention every time.

Why This Lesson Matters More Than You Think

If you remember only one thing from this chapter, make it this:

Markets don't reward intelligence. They reward behavior that fits the incentives.

Which means strategy is less about outsmarting people and more about understanding what makes their choices predictable.

Once you see predictability clearly:

- You can design around it

- Signal into it

- Or occasionally, break it

But you can't ignore it.

Because rational doesn't mean smart.

It means repeatable.

And repeatable behavior, once noticed, becomes exploitable.

Which brings us to the next problem.

People don't just act.

They signal.

And most brands are shouting things they never meant to say.

Marker's still squeaking. Let's talk about signals.

CHAPTER THREE
Every Strategy Is a Bet,
Even the Safe Ones

There is a comforting myth in marketing that goes something like this:

"We're not gambling. We're being careful."

Careful is a lovely word. It sounds responsible. Adult. Board-approved.

It is also, very often, a lie.

Because the moment you choose a path in a world where other people respond, you've placed a bet. You may not have rolled dice, but you've absolutely pushed chips forward.

Game theory just has the decency to admit it.

The Myth of the Risk-Free Move

Somewhere in every organization lives a belief that there exists a strategy so sensible, so conservative, so thoroughly researched that it carries no risk at all.

Usually it's called:

- "Following best practice"
- "Waiting to see"
- "Let's not be first"
- or "We'll revisit this next quarter"

These aren't neutral moves. They are choices with payoffs.

Waiting is a bet that nothing important changes.

Copying is a bet that sameness won't be punished.

Incrementalism is a bet that the category won't move without you.

Sometimes those bets win. Often they quietly compound losses.

Safety Is Just a Bet with a Smaller Story

Here's what game theory makes uncomfortably clear:

There are no non-moves.

Not launching is a signal.

Not responding is a signal.

Not changing price is a signal.

Not taking a position is a position.

The market doesn't freeze while you deliberate. Competitors don't pause. Customers don't stop learning.

So when teams say, "This is the safe option," what they usually mean is:

"This is the option that makes us least uncomfortable right now."

Comfort is not a strategy. It's a mood.

Why Conservative Moves Invite Aggressive Responses

One of the oddities of strategic environments is that caution can attract aggression.

When you hesitate:

- Competitors test your boundaries
- Customers experiment with alternatives
- Partners renegotiate leverage

Game theory explains why. Safe moves often reveal:

- Fear of loss
- Reluctance to commit
- A desire to avoid conflict

Those are not moral flaws. They are signals.

And signals invite response.

The more visible your caution, the more tempting it becomes for others to push.

The Whiteboard Bet

On the whiteboard, I draw a simple table.

Two columns:

- "What we hope happens"
- "What happens if we're wrong"

Most strategies die in the second column.

Teams love to discuss upside. They rarely dwell on downside in concrete terms. Downside stays abstract, vague, and politely ignored.

Game theory insists you stare at it.

Because rational players don't just look at expected gains. They look at exposure.

And exposure is where "safe" strategies often turn out to be reckless.

Loss Aversion: The Quiet Puppet Master

There's a psychological engine humming under all of this.

People hate losing more than they love winning.

Which means strategies are often designed not to win, but to avoid blame.

- "At least we didn't overspend."
- "At least we didn't rock the boat."
- "At least we did what everyone else did."

Game theory doesn't judge this instinct. It models it. And then it shows you the cost.

When everyone plays to avoid loss, no one plays to shape outcomes. The game stagnates. Equilibrium sets in. Differentiation erodes.

The industry becomes safe, predictable, and vulnerable.

The Graybeard Rule About Bets

Here's the rule experience eventually writes on your whiteboard for you:

The question is never whether you're betting.

The question is whether you understand the bet you're making.

Are you betting on:

- Competitors staying put?
- Customers not learning?
- Timing saving you?
- History repeating?

Those bets may be reasonable. But pretending they're not bets is how organizations get blindsided.

Choosing Your Risk on Purpose

Good strategy doesn't eliminate risk.

It chooses risk.

It decides:

- Where to be bold
- Where to be boring
- Where to commit
- Where to remain flexible

Game theory gives you the lens to see these choices clearly, instead of hiding them under the word "safe."

Because once you admit every move is a wager, something liberating happens.

You stop asking, "Is this risky?"

And start asking, "Is this the risk we want?"

Now that we've accepted we're betting whether we like it or not, the next problem shows up fast:

People don't just respond to what you do.

They respond to what they think it means.

Which brings us to the loudest, slipperiest part of strategy. Signals.

CHAPTER FOUR

Marketing Is Mostly About What People Think Other People Think

If you want to watch a room of smart marketers get uncomfortable, ask a simple question:

"Why does this work?"

The first answers usually involve features, benefits, and targeting. The real answer, the one nobody says out loud right away, is usually this:

Because people believe other people believe it.

That's not cynicism. That's game theory with a pulse.

The Second-Order Problem Nobody Budgets For

Most marketing plans are built on first-order thinking:

- What do we want customers to think?
- How do we position ourselves?
- What message will resonate?

Game theory pushes one level deeper:

- What do customers think other customers think?
- What do competitors think customers think?
- What does everyone think this move signals?

That second-order layer is where strategy actually lives.

You don't buy a brand only because you like it.

You buy it because it fits how you expect others to see you.

You don't fear a competitor because of what they did.

You fear what their move implies about what they might do next.

Beliefs about beliefs shape behavior far more than facts.

Why Perception Moves Faster Than Reality

Reality is slow.

Belief is agile.

A product can be unchanged while perception shifts overnight. A brand can lose ground without losing a single feature. A price can feel expensive even when it isn't.

Game theory explains why: beliefs update asymmetrically.

People notice signals faster than substance.

- A price cut signals weakness or confidence, depending on context
- A redesign signals change, whether or not change exists
- Silence signals indecision, even when it's strategic

Once beliefs shift, behavior follows. Reality scrambles to catch up.

The Whiteboard Spiral

On the whiteboard, I draw a loop:

Beliefs → Actions → Observed Outcomes → Updated Beliefs

Then I draw arrows pointing everywhere, because that's how it actually works.

Marketing loves linear stories. Markets don't cooperate.

When you launch something:

- Customers act
- Competitors interpret
- Analysts speculate
- Sales teams explain
- The category narrative mutates

And suddenly you're responding not to what you did, but to what people think it means.

That spiral doesn't wait for clarity. It feeds on inference.

Why Categories Are Shared Hallucinations

A category is not a fact. It's a collective agreement.

Everyone agrees on:

- What "premium" looks like
- What "value" signals
- What "innovative" sounds like
- What "risky" feels like

Those agreements aren't written down. They're enforced socially.

When a brand violates them, it doesn't fail because the product is wrong. It fails because the belief system rejects it.

Game theory treats categories as coordination games. Once a shared belief exists, deviating becomes costly, even if you're right.

That's why changing perception is harder than changing features.

Why Explaining Rarely Works

When beliefs are at stake, explanation is a weak tool.

You can't out-explain:

- A competitor's framing
- A viral interpretation
- A pricing signal
- A poorly timed move

Game theory is ruthless about this.

Beliefs are not updated by intent. They are updated by observed behavior and how that behavior fits existing narratives.

Which is why:

- Rebrands fail when actions don't follow
- Apologies ring hollow without consequence
- "Trust us" never works as a slogan

The Graybeard Rule About Beliefs

Write this one down too:

You don't compete on what you mean.

You compete on what others infer.

Once you accept that, strategy changes:

- You design moves that are legible
- You avoid cleverness that requires explanation
- You think about how actions will be retold

Because marketing is not a private conversation. It's a public game of interpretation.

Setting Up the Next Problem

Beliefs don't float freely. They're shaped by cues.

Price. Packaging. Timing. Silence. Speed.

All of them speak.

Most of them speak louder than your copy.

Game theory has a word for this: signals.

And most brands are sending far more of them than they realize.

Marker's squeaking again.

After the break let's talk about what you're accidentally saying.

CHAPTER FIVE
Signals, Not Slogans

If marketing were judged by what it said, most brands would be geniuses.

Unfortunately, markets listen to what brands do.

Game theory calls these actions signals. Marketers usually call them "details," right up until those details set the narrative on fire.

Why Words Are the Quietest Thing You Do

Slogans are polite.

Signals are loud.

You can say "premium" all day long.

Your pricing, distribution, response time, and discount behavior will contradict you by lunch.

You can say "customer first."

Your return policy, onboarding friction, and support scripts will deliver the verdict.

Game theory doesn't privilege intention. It privileges observable behavior.

Because behavior is costly. Words are cheap.

The Signal Stack Nobody Audits

Every brand sends signals whether it means to or not.

Some are obvious:

- Price changes
- Product launches
- Promotions
- Partnerships

Others are quieter but deadlier:

- How often you discount
- How quickly you respond
- Where you show up and where you don't
- What you ignore

The problem isn't bad signals.

It's inconsistent signals.

In game theory, consistency is credibility. In marketing, inconsistency is confusion.

The Whiteboard Exercise That Makes People Squirm

On the whiteboard, I write:

What we say   What we do   Space

Then I leave space.

This is where the room goes quiet.

Because when you line them up side by side, the gaps start talking.

"We say we're premium."

"We discount every quarter."

"We say we're innovative."

"We copy competitors six months later."

"We say we're long-term partners."

"We renegotiate at the first sign of pressure."

None of these are moral failings. They are strategic contradictions.

Game theory doesn't scold them. It explains the outcome.

Signals Only Matter If They Cost Something

Here's a simple rule that separates noise from signal:

If it's cheap to say, it's cheap to ignore.

Anyone can promise.

Not everyone can commit.

That's why:

- High prices signal confidence
- Long warranties signal belief
- Limited availability signals restraint
- Slow, deliberate moves can signal control

Costly signals are credible because they hurt if you're wrong.

Which is also why fake confidence collapses so quickly. The costs catch up.

When Silence Screams

One of the most misunderstood signals is silence.

Silence can mean:

- Confidence
- Indifference
- Confusion
- Fear

The market decides which one it means.

In game theory, silence is never neutral. It is interpreted in context, through existing beliefs, and updated instantly.

Brands that go quiet during change invite others to explain the silence for them.

And they will.

Why Clever Signals Backfire

Marketers love cleverness. Game theory does not.

Signals work best when they're obvious. When they require explanation, they lose power.

If your positioning needs a footnote, it's already in trouble.

The market doesn't reward nuance. It rewards legibility.

The Graybeard Rule About Signals

Here it is:

Every move you make teaches the market how to treat you next time.

Discount once, you've taught patience.

Respond slowly, you've taught escalation.

Overreact, you've taught provocation.

Signals are lessons. Lessons compound.

Which is why the best strategies often look boring in isolation. They're designed to teach the right lessons over time.

What Comes Next

Signals don't exist in a vacuum.

They pile up.

They repeat.

They form reputations.

And reputation, in a repeated game, changes everything.

So far we've been talking about single moves.

Next, we'll talk about what happens when the market remembers.

Marker down.

Time to talk about credibility.

CHAPTER SIX
Credibility Is the Only Currency That Doesn't Inflate

Most things in marketing depreciate.

Claims get copied.

Features get matched.

Attention gets expensive.

Credibility, on the other hand, compounds.

Game theory treats credibility not as a virtue, but as a strategic asset. Once earned, it changes how every future move is interpreted. Once lost, even good moves are questioned.

Marketers tend to talk about trust. Game theory talks about belief stability.

Same idea. Less romance.

Why the Market Keeps Score Longer Than You Do

Organizations have short memories. Markets do not.

Customers remember:

- How you behaved during a shortage
- What happened when something went wrong
- Whether your promises survived pressure

Competitors remember too.

- Who bluffs
- Who follows through
- Who panics
- Who holds the line

Game theory calls this a repeated game. What you do today affects how tomorrow's move is received.

Marketing often acts like every launch is a first date. The market treats it like a long marriage with receipts.

Credibility Is Built in Boring Moments

Here's the inconvenient truth:

Credibility is rarely built during big campaigns.

It's built when:

- You don't discount, even though you could
- You keep prices steady when costs rise
- You fix a problem without turning it into a press release
- You say "no" and mean it

These moments don't trend. They don't win awards. They do teach the market how seriously to take you.

Game theory predicts this. Consistent behavior across repeated interactions becomes a reliable signal.

Reliability becomes power.

The Whiteboard Line You Don't Want to Cross

On the whiteboard, I draw a line.

Above it: Credible

Below it: Questioned

Once you cross that line, everything costs more.

- Discounts must be deeper
- Proof must be louder
- Promises must be repeated
- Silence is interpreted negatively

This is why once-trusted brands struggle to regain footing. The game didn't reset. It remembered.

Credibility, unlike awareness, is not easily bought back.

Why Empty Promises Are Strategically Expensive

In the short term, overpromising feels efficient. It accelerates attention. It wins early rounds.

In a repeated game, it's radioactive.

Game theory shows that players who defect early may win once, but lose cooperation permanently. Trust collapses. Future interactions become defensive.

In marketing terms:

- Customers demand guarantees
- Partners hedge
- Competitors test boundaries

The system becomes hostile because it learned to be.

Consistency Beats Brilliance Over Time

This is where graybeards nod quietly.

Brilliant moves are memorable.

Consistent behavior is decisive.

Game theory doesn't reward creativity in isolation. It rewards patterns that others can rely on.

That's why:

- Steady brands command premiums
- Predictable partners get better terms
- Calm competitors are taken seriously

Consistency reduces uncertainty. Reduced uncertainty lowers resistance.

The Graybeard Rule About Credibility

Write this one carefully:

You don't earn credibility by saying the right thing once.

You earn it by doing the same thing when it would be easier not to.

That's when the market updates its beliefs.

And once beliefs stabilize, your future moves carry more weight with less effort.

Setting Up the Next Shift

Up to now, we've been talking about individual moves and signals.

But something strange happens once credibility and repetition enter the picture.

Games stop being about winning each round.

They become about where the game settles.

Industries stabilize.

Norms emerge.

Everyone looks around and says, "This is just how it works."

Game theory has a name for that resting place.

Marketers call it best practice.

Next, we're going to talk about equilibrium.

And why it's where bad ideas go to rest.

CHAPTER SEVEN

The Comfortable Stalemate Everyone Calls "Best Practice"

There is a moment in every mature industry when innovation slows, differentiation blurs, and everyone starts using the same words with slightly different fonts.

Marketing calls this best practice.

Game theory calls it equilibrium.

Same thing. Very different tone.

How Smart Industries Get Stuck

Equilibrium happens when no player can improve their situation by changing their behavior alone.

Read that again. Slowly.

It doesn't mean the outcome is good.

It doesn't mean customers are happy.

It doesn't mean margins are healthy.

It just means that moving first feels dangerous.

So nobody does.

Everyone watches everyone else. Everyone maintains the same pricing bands, feature sets, messaging tropes, and channel mix. Deviations are punished quickly. Conformity is rewarded quietly.

From the inside, it feels responsible.

From the outside, it looks like paralysis with a budget.

The Whiteboard Graveyard

On the whiteboard, I draw a neat row of logos.

Same colors.

Same promises.

Same claims of differentiation that require a sales rep to explain.

This is what equilibrium looks like in the wild.

No one planned it.

No one voted for it.

Everyone contributed.

Game theory explains why. When the cost of deviation is immediate and visible, and the benefit is uncertain and delayed, rational players stay put.

Safety wins. Creativity waits.

Why Best Practice Is So Seductive

Best practice has excellent PR.

It sounds:

- Proven
- Defensible
- Professional
- Career-safe

If it fails, you didn't fail. The industry did.

That's the real appeal.

Game theory doesn't care about career safety. It cares about incentives. And incentives reward conformity far more often than they reward distinction.

Which is how equilibrium becomes self-reinforcing.

The Punishment Mechanism Nobody Mentions

Equilibria persist because deviation is punished.

- Lower prices trigger retaliation
- New features get copied
- New messages get reframed
- New channels get flooded

The market teaches a clear lesson:

"Don't try that again."

Most brands learn it quickly.

Game theory doesn't see this as hostility. It sees it as coordination. Players enforcing shared expectations so the system stays stable.

Stability is comfortable. Comfort is dangerous.

Why Customers Don't Save You

There's a popular fantasy that customers will rescue differentiation.

They won't.

Customers adapt to equilibrium just like companies do. They learn how the category works. They adjust expectations. They optimize behavior.

That's how:

- Promotions become expected
- Loyalty erodes
- Switching costs vanish
- Trust thins

From the customer's point of view, equilibrium is efficient.

From the brand's point of view, it's suffocating.

The Graybeard Rule About Equilibrium

Here it is, and it stings a little:

If everyone agrees this is "just how the category works," you're already in trouble.

Equilibrium is not the end state of good strategy. It's the result of strategy avoidance.

It's where ambition goes to nap.

Escaping Without Getting Shot

Breaking equilibrium is risky. Game theory never pretends otherwise.

The mistake is thinking the only options are:

- Stay put forever
- Or blow everything up

There are ways to shift the game without declaring war. But they require patience, credibility, and a willingness to look odd for a while.

That's what the next chapter is about.

Because if equilibrium is where bad ideas rest, then the real strategic question becomes:

How do you move the game without becoming the cautionary tale?

Marker back in hand.

Let's talk about breaking the pattern.

CHAPTER EIGHT

Breaking the Pattern Without Blowing Yourself Up

Every strategist eventually reaches the same fork in the road.

On one side:

Stay in equilibrium. Blend in. Compete on execution and endurance.

On the other:

Do something different and risk becoming the case study nobody wants to present.

Most books make this sound heroic. Game theory makes it sound honest.

Breaking a pattern is not bravery. It's calculated disruption with a long memory.

Why Most "Bold Moves" Fail Loudly

The graveyard of strategy is full of boldness without preparation.

Brands leap out of equilibrium by:

- Slashing prices with no exit plan
- Repositioning without permission from the market
- Launching innovations customers didn't ask for
- Declaring themselves "different" without acting differently

Game theory predicts the outcome.

The system reacts.

Competitors punish.

Customers hesitate.

Internal nerves fray.

Not because the idea was wrong, but because the move wasn't credible.

The Difference Between Change and Shock

Markets tolerate change. They punish shock.

Change:

- Is legible
- Builds on existing beliefs
- Signals intention clearly
- Allows others to update expectations gradually

Shock:

- Violates norms without explanation
- Breaks trust before building proof
- Forces others into defensive posture

Game theory favors the first. Marketers often accidentally choose the second.

The Whiteboard Test for Pattern Breaking

On the whiteboard, I draw three boxes:

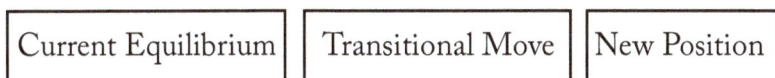

Current Equilibrium	Transitional Move	New Position

Most failed strategies skip the middle box.

They jump straight from "what is" to "what we wish were true" and hope momentum fills the gap.

Game theory is merciless here. Players don't update beliefs that fast. They need evidence. Repetition. Consistency.

The middle is where credibility is earned or lost.

The Power of Asymmetric Moves

One way out of equilibrium is asymmetry.

Instead of competing where everyone is strong, you shift where competition is awkward.

- You compete on time instead of price

- You compete on simplicity instead of features

- You compete on commitment instead of flexibility

- You compete on restraint instead of abundance

Asymmetric moves work because they're hard to copy without self-harm.

Game theory loves asymmetry. Copying is rational only when it's cheap.

Why Small Moves Often Matter More Than Big Ones

Breaking equilibrium doesn't require spectacle. It requires persistence.

Small, repeated deviations:

- Teach the market what to expect

- Reframe norms gradually

- Avoid triggering full retaliation

Big moves attract attention. Small moves change expectations.

Graybeards learn this the slow way.

The Cost of Looking Wrong Before Looking Right

Here's the part nobody puts in the deck.

When you break a pattern, you will look wrong before you look right.

Competitors will mock.

Analysts will question.

Internal teams will whisper.

Game theory calls this the out-of-equilibrium penalty.

It's real. It's uncomfortable. And it's unavoidable.

The question isn't whether you can avoid it. It's whether you can endure it long enough for beliefs to update.

The Graybeard Rule About Change

Write this one carefully:

If your new strategy looks instantly sensible to everyone, you didn't change the game.

Real shifts feel awkward at first. They contradict expectations. They require explanation through action, not slides.

That's the price of escape.

Setting Up the Next Phase

So far, we've talked about:

- Single moves
- Signals
- Credibility
- Equilibrium
- Pattern breaking

All of that matters.

But everything changes once the game repeats long enough for memory to matter more than momentum.

That's where loyalty, reputation, and retaliation enter the picture.

Next, we move from one-off moves to ongoing relationships.

From breaking patterns…to playing the long game.

CHAPTER NINE
First Movers, Fast Followers, and the Myth of Advantage

Every industry has its folklore.

One of the loudest legends goes like this:

"If we get there first, we win."

Game theory raises an eyebrow and asks, "Win what, exactly?"

Because being first is not an advantage. It's a position. And positions only become advantages if others can't easily take them away.

Why First Feels Powerful *(and Often Isn't)*

Being first gets attention.

Attention feels like momentum.

Momentum feels like inevitability.

None of those are defenses.

First movers teach the market:

- What the category is
- What's possible
- What mistakes to avoid

Fast followers show up with cleaner messaging, fewer scars, and a sharpened sense of what customers will tolerate.

Game theory explains this simply: early moves reveal information. Information is valuable to everyone else.

Being first often means being generous.

The Whiteboard Timeline Illusion

On the whiteboard, I draw a timeline.

The first mover sits at the left, proudly labeled "Innovator."

A follower appears later, labeled "Copycat."

Then I erase the labels.

Because markets don't reward originality. They reward coordination.

Customers don't care who arrived first. They care who fits the story they already understand.

Once a category stabilizes, the memory of "who was first" fades fast. What remains is who feels reliable.

When First Mover Advantage Actually Exists

Game theory isn't anti-first. It's anti-naïve.

First mover advantage exists when:

- Switching costs are high
- Standards are set early
- Network effects lock in behavior
- Learning curves are steep and protected

Absent those conditions, first movers are scouts, not settlers.

They map the terrain. Others build houses.

Why Fast Followers Aren't Cowards

Fast followers are often framed as timid. In reality, they are practicing informed restraint.

They let:

- Early confusion resolve
- Customer language form
- Failure points surface

Then they move with clarity.

Game theory calls this strategic patience. Marketing calls it "lacking vision." History usually sides with patience.

The Real Advantage: Moving Second on Purpose

The graybeard trick is not being first or second.

It's choosing when information matters more than speed.

Moving second lets you:

- Avoid signaling desperation
- Enter with credibility
- Break equilibrium intelligently

The mistake is drifting into second place by accident.

Intentional timing is strategy. Hesitation is not.

The Graybeard Rule About Timing

Here it is:

Speed without insulation is just exposure.

Being early without protection invites imitation. Being late without differentiation invites irrelevance.

Game theory teaches that timing is valuable only when paired with structure.

Where This Leaves Us

By now, a pattern should be emerging.

- Strategy is interactive
- Behavior is predictable
- Signals teach
- Credibility compounds
- Equilibrium traps
- Change requires patience
- Timing is contextual

Which brings us to the most important shift of all.

Up to now, we've treated strategy as a sequence of moves.

Next, we treat it as a relationship.

Because once the game repeats, the goal is no longer winning the round.

It's shaping how the game is played.

Turn the page.

We're about to talk about loyalty, memory, and why the long game quietly beats the loud one.

CHAPTER 10

Why Loyalty Programs Work
(And Why Most Don't)

Loyalty programs sound noble.

"Reward our best customers."

"Build relationships."

"Create community."

Game theory squints and asks a simpler question:

What behavior are you training?

Because loyalty, in a repeated game, is not about affection. It's about incentives, memory, and expectation.

Loyalty Is Not Love. It's Predictability.

Customers do not stay because they feel warm feelings toward a brand. They stay because leaving feels inconvenient, risky, or unnecessary.

Game theory calls this path dependence.

Once people invest time, points, habits, or identity, switching stops being neutral. It becomes a decision with friction.

Good loyalty programs understand this. Bad ones confuse rewards with relationships.

The Whiteboard Loyalty Loop

On the whiteboard, I draw a loop:

Behavior → Reward → Expectation → Future Behavior

Most loyalty programs break at step three.

They reward behavior but forget that rewards become expectations. Expectations harden fast. What once delighted becomes table stakes.

Game theory predicts this perfectly. Repeated rewards reset the baseline.

Discount-driven loyalty doesn't create commitment. It creates patience.

Why Points Programs Teach the Wrong Lesson

Points are easy to count. They're also easy to exploit.

When loyalty is framed purely as accumulation:

- Customers optimize for points, not value

- Engagement becomes transactional

- Switching happens as soon as the math changes

You didn't build loyalty. You built a spreadsheet rivalry.

Game theory treats this as rational behavior. Customers are responding to incentives exactly as designed.

The failure is not theirs.

Real Loyalty Is About Future Belief

Effective loyalty programs do one thing well:

They change what customers believe will happen next time.

- Will the brand remember me?

- Will problems be handled fairly?

- Will consistency be rewarded?

- Will mistakes be forgiven?

These beliefs shape repeat behavior more than any coupon.

Which is why service recovery often creates more loyalty than flawless execution.

When Loyalty Becomes a Trap

There's a dark side.

Once customers believe you rely on loyalty programs to retain them, they start negotiating harder.

- "I've been with you for years…"

- "Other brands are offering more…"

- "What can you do for me?"

Game theory again: repeated interactions shift bargaining power.

Loyalty must be mutual. If only one side feels committed, the game turns extractive.

The Graybeard Rule About Loyalty

Here it is:

Loyalty is not what customers feel.

It's what they expect will happen if they stay.

Design for expectation, not applause.

If your program teaches customers to wait, bargain, or churn strategically, it's working perfectly. Just not for you.

What Comes Next

Loyalty is one piece of the long game.

The next piece is reputation.

Not what you claim.

Not what you advertise.

What the market remembers when you're not in the room.

And memory, in game theory, is where power starts to show up.

Marker back in hand.

Let's talk about reputation.

Chapter Eleven

Reputation Is Just Memory at Scale

If loyalty is personal, reputation is communal.

You can disappoint one customer and recover.

Disappoint a pattern of customers and the market remembers for you.

Game theory treats reputation as a shared memory system. Marketing tends to treat it like a press problem.

Only one of those interpretations holds up over time.

Reputation Exists Even When You're Quiet

Here's the uncomfortable part.

You don't get to choose whether you have a reputation.

You only influence what it becomes.

Silence doesn't reset memory. It lets others fill it in.

Customers talk. Partners compare notes. Competitors infer intentions. Algorithms amplify signals without asking what you meant.

Game theory assumes information spreads. Marketing sometimes hopes it won't.

Hope is not a strategy.

The Whiteboard Memory Test

On the whiteboard, I write one question:

"What does the market expect us to do under pressure?"

That answer is your reputation.

Not your tagline.

Not your mission statement.

Your behavior when things get inconvenient.

Game theory predicts that once expectations stabilize, behavior becomes self-fulfilling.

If you're known for folding, people push.

If you're known for fairness, people cooperate.

If you're known for volatility, people hedge.

Why Reputation Changes the Rules

Reputation alters payoffs.

A credible brand doesn't need to explain every move.

A shaky one must over-signal constantly.

This is why:

- Trusted brands survive mistakes
- Distrusted brands need perfection
- Calm brands set terms
- Reactive brands chase narratives

Game theory shows this clearly. In repeated games, reputation acts as a shortcut. It reduces uncertainty and speeds decisions.

Markets love shortcuts.

The Cost of Inconsistent Behavior

Reputation is not built by averages. It's built by extremes.

One panicked move can outweigh ten calm ones. One broken promise can undo years of consistency.

Game theory doesn't find this unfair. It finds it efficient. Extreme signals carry more information.

This is why:

- Price volatility damages trust
- Erratic messaging confuses partners
- Overreaction invites testing

The market updates beliefs aggressively.

Reputation Is Hard to Fake and Easy to Spend

You can borrow credibility once or twice. After that, the bill arrives.

Promotions that contradict positioning.

Apologies without consequence.

Promises made under pressure.

Each one spends reputation capital.

Game theory teaches restraint. Marketing often teaches amplification.

Only one of those survives long games.

The Graybeard Rule About Reputation

Write this one slowly:

Your reputation is the answer people give when you're not in the room.

You don't manage it with campaigns. You manage it with choices.

And once the market agrees on that answer, changing it requires sustained, visible behavior over time.

Not announcements.

Where This Leaves Us

At this point, something important has shifted.

We're no longer talking about:

- Individual tactics
- Clever moves
- Tactical wins

We're talking about structure.

Reputation shapes structure. Loyalty reinforces it. Equilibrium hardens it.

Which raises the next uncomfortable question:

If behavior creates the game, can we design the game instead of fighting inside it?

That's where real leverage lives.

CHAPTER TWELVE

Punishment, Forgiveness, and Knowing When to Let It Go

Every strategist eventually learns this the hard way:

Markets remember slights longer than intentions.

Game theory doesn't romanticize this. It explains it.

In repeated games, behavior is not just observed. It's judged, stored, and acted upon later. Sometimes immediately. Sometimes when you least expect it.

Why Retaliation Feels Good and Backfires Quietly

When someone undercuts your price, copies your feature, or poaches your customer, the instinct is immediate.

"Respond."

Game theory doesn't forbid retaliation. It just insists you understand the cost.

Punishment teaches the market two things:

- You noticed
- You're willing to escalate

That can deter future attacks. It can also invite them.

Escalation changes the game from competition to conflict. Once there, everyone's payoff shrinks.

The Whiteboard Retaliation Ladder

On the whiteboard, I draw a ladder:

Ignore → Signal → Respond → Punish → Escalate

Most brands jump rungs.

They skip signaling and go straight to punishment. The market doesn't read that as strength. It reads it as volatility.

Game theory favors proportionate response. Not because it's polite, but because it stabilizes expectations.

Forgiveness Is Strategic, Not Soft

Forgiveness has terrible branding.

It sounds weak. Passive. Naïve.

Game theory disagrees.

In repeated interactions, forgiveness resets cooperation faster than domination. It signals confidence and long-term orientation.

This is why:

- Fair dispute resolution builds loyalty
- Calm responses earn respect
- Selective memory outperforms grudges

Forgiveness is not forgetting. It's choosing not to escalate when escalation would damage future payoffs.

When Letting Go Is the Smart Move

Not every provocation deserves a response.

Some competitors want attention.

Some customers want leverage.

Some conflicts are traps.

Game theory introduces the idea of strategic silence.

If responding teaches the wrong lesson, don't teach it.

Ignoring is not surrender. It's refusing to change the game in someone else's favor.

The Danger of Overreaction

Overreaction teaches the market:

- You're sensitive
- You're reactive

- You can be baited

Once learned, this behavior gets tested repeatedly.

Game theory shows this pattern clearly. Players probe for weaknesses. Overreaction is a flashing signal.

Calm is underrated. Predictability is power.

The Graybeard Rule About Conflict

Here it is:

Not every move deserves a counter-move.

Sometimes the smartest response is no response at all.

Other times, it's a small, visible, proportional one that resets expectations without inviting war.

The goal is not to win every exchange. It's to preserve the game you want to keep playing.

What Comes Next

Up to now, we've been focused outward.

Competitors. Customers. Markets.

Next, we turn inward.

Because some of the fiercest games are not between brands, but inside them.

Incentives collide. Metrics distort. Departments compete.

And suddenly the strategy loses to itself.

Marker down.

After the break it's time to talk about micro choices and macro behavior.

CHAPTER THIRTEEN

Small Decisions, Big Ripples

If you want to understand why good strategies fail, stop looking at the strategy.

Start looking at the incentives.

Game theory has a long, unglamorous obsession with this truth: systems don't behave the way leaders intend. They behave the way incentives reward.

Marketing departments like to believe they're aligned. Game theory has seen better.

The Invisible Games Inside the Organization

Every organization is a bundle of smaller games pretending to be one.

Sales wants volume.

Marketing wants positioning.

Finance wants predictability.

Product wants features.

Leadership wants harmony.

None of these goals are wrong. Together, they are combustible.

Game theory explains why. Each group responds rationally to its own payoffs. The result is not coordination. It's interference.

The Whiteboard Incentive Map

On the whiteboard, I draw boxes labeled by department.

Then I draw arrows to what they're rewarded for.

This is where the room gets honest.

Discounting suddenly makes sense.

Short-term campaigns stop looking mysterious.

Brand erosion becomes predictable.

Nobody is sabotaging strategy. They're optimizing locally.

Game theory calls this a coordination failure. Marketers call it "alignment issues."

Why Metrics Lie Without Meaning To

Metrics are not evil. They are persuasive.

People do what they're measured on, even when the measurement distorts reality.

- Clicks beat comprehension
- Leads beat loyalty
- Volume beats margin
- Speed beats quality

Game theory predicts this perfectly. When rewards are narrow, behavior narrows with them.

The tragedy is not bad people. It's precise incentives.

Small Choices Compound Fast

A single discount feels harmless.

A single exception feels humane.

A single workaround feels efficient.

In isolation, they are.

In repetition, they reshape the game.

Customers learn patterns.

Sales learns boundaries.

Partners learn leverage.

Small decisions don't stay small. They teach.

Why Culture Is Just Incentives with a Long Memory

Culture is not values on a wall.

It's the accumulated memory of which behaviors got rewarded, tolerated, or ignored.

Game theory treats culture as a long-running equilibrium. It persists not because it's loved, but because deviating is costly.

Change incentives and culture follows. Talk about culture without changing incentives and nothing moves.

The Graybeard Rule About Systems

Here it is:

If you don't design the incentives, the system will design them for you.

And it will not consult the strategy deck.

Setting Up the Next Turn

We've now seen how:

- External games shape markets
- Internal games shape outcomes
- Incentives quietly override intention

This leads to a sobering realization.

Sometimes, the biggest competitor is not across the table.

It's across the hallway.

Next, we're going to talk about structure. About platforms, ecosystems, and how some companies stop competing move by move and start shaping the board itself.

Marker uncapped.

Let's zoom out.

CHAPTER FOURTEEN
Designing the Game
Instead of Winning It

There comes a point in every competitive environment when trying to "win" harder stops working.

You optimize.

You execute.

You improve margins by basis points and morale by slogans.

And still, the game feels rigged.

Game theory suggests a heretical alternative:

Stop trying to win the game. Start designing it.

Why the Biggest Wins Don't Look Like Wins at First

When companies truly change their fortunes, it often doesn't look like competition.

It looks like:

- Redefining the category
- Creating new roles for participants
- Changing how value flows
- Making certain behaviors easier and others expensive

Competitors don't panic immediately. They hesitate.

That hesitation is the signal something structural just changed.

The Whiteboard Board

On the whiteboard, I stop drawing competitors.

I draw:

- Customers

- Partners
- Channels
- Rules
- Frictions

Then I ask a dangerous question:

"Who benefits from the game working exactly as it does today?"

Because the answer is rarely "the customer." And almost never "the challenger."

Game theory teaches that power flows to those who set constraints, not those who play hardest inside them.

Platforms Are Not Products. They're Invitations.

Platforms succeed because they invite others into the game.

They:

- Reward participation
- Lower friction for some behaviors
- Raise friction for others
- Create switching costs that feel like convenience

Game theory sees platforms as coordination engines. Once enough players commit, leaving becomes irrational.

Marketing often sees platforms as features.

That misunderstanding is expensive.

Ecosystems Beat Campaigns

Campaigns spike attention. Ecosystems accumulate advantage.

An ecosystem:

- Teaches partners how to behave
- Teaches customers what to expect
- Teaches competitors where not to go

Game theory predicts this stability. Once behavior coordinates around a structure, individual tactics matter less.

That's when competition feels unfair.

It is.

Why Rule-Setters Look Calm

The calmest players are often the most powerful.

They don't react quickly. They don't chase trends. They don't shout.

They let the structure do the work.

Game theory explains this beautifully. When you design incentives correctly, others enforce them for you.

Which is why platforms rarely argue with participants. They adjust terms.

The Graybeard Rule About Power

Here it is:

If you're fighting every battle, you're not controlling the terrain.

Real leverage comes from shaping defaults, not winning debates.

The Risk of Playing Architect Too Soon

Designing the game is not a shortcut.

It requires:

- Credibility
- Patience
- Tolerance for slow adoption
- Willingness to be misunderstood

Most organizations try to architect before they've earned trust. The result looks arrogant instead of visionary.

Game theory is unforgiving here. Coordination requires belief.

Where This Leaves Us

We've moved from:

- Moves
- To patterns
- To systems
- To structure

Which brings us to the final internal challenge.

Once you start shaping the game, your biggest risk is not competition.

It's your own organization losing the plot.

Next, we talk about data, dashboards, and how metrics can quietly sabotage strategy while smiling politely.

Marker down.

Tuesday let's talk about numbers.

Chapter Fifteen
When Data Lies
and Incentives Confess

There was a time when strategy meetings involved arguments, opinions, and the occasional raised eyebrow.

Then dashboards arrived.

Suddenly, nobody argued anymore. They just pointed.

Numbers have a way of ending conversations, even when they shouldn't.

Game theory doesn't distrust data. It distrusts how humans behave once data becomes the referee.

Data Doesn't Decide. People Respond to It.

Data feels objective. Clean. Unemotional.

People are not.

The moment a metric becomes important, behavior bends around it like gravity showed up late to the meeting.

Clicks increase.

Quality drops.

Leads soar.

Conversion sinks.

Everyone celebrates.

Game theory predicted this before dashboards had fonts.

People optimize for what's measured, not what's meant.

The Whiteboard Metric Trap

On the whiteboard, I write two columns:

What we measure

What actually matters

Then I wait.

This is where the nervous laughter starts.

Because everyone can see the gap:

- Engagement versus understanding
- Reach versus relevance
- Speed versus trust
- Efficiency versus durability

Metrics don't lie maliciously. They lie by omission.

They tell you what moved, not what it taught.

Why KPIs Create Shadow Strategies

When incentives attach to numbers, unofficial strategies emerge.

Sales learns which deals count.

Marketing learns which campaigns look good.

Product learns which features get shipped fastest.

None of this requires bad actors. It requires clarity.

Game theory calls these local optima. Everyone improves their slice while the whole stagnates.

From the outside, it looks like confusion. From the inside, it's perfectly rational behavior.

The Seduction of Precision

Dashboards make uncertainty look tidy.

Decimals imply control. Trends imply causation. Graphs imply inevitability.

Game theory waves a hand and says, "Careful."

In strategic environments, measurement changes the environment. Observing behavior alters behavior.

Which means yesterday's data often describes a game that no longer exists.

When Data Becomes the Game

The real danger arrives when success is defined entirely by metrics.

At that point:

- The strategy serves the dashboard
- The dashboard replaces judgment
- And long-term outcomes become externalities

Customers feel this immediately.

Competitors exploit it eventually.

Organizations deny it loudly.

Game theory is unmoved. The incentives arc doing exactly what they were told.

The Graybeard Rule About Numbers

Write this one where the dashboard can see it:

If a metric becomes a target, it stops being a measure.

Numbers are inputs to thinking, not substitutes for it.

Good strategists use data to inform decisions. Poor ones let data decide for them.

Pulling the Threads Together

At this point, the throughline should be clear.

- Strategy is interactive
- Behavior follows incentives
- Signals teach
- Memory compounds
- Equilibrium traps
- Structure creates leverage
- Metrics shape behavior

Game theory isn't abstract. It's descriptive.

It explains why smart people, good intentions, and powerful tools still produce predictable mistakes.

And that brings us to the final stretch.

Not tactics.

Not frameworks.

But discipline.

Next, we close with the practical habits that keep strategists from forgetting all of this the moment the next dashboard refreshes.

Marker capped.

One last class to go.

CHAPTER SIXTEEN

Five Questions to Ask Before You Launch Anything

This is the chapter the graybeard writes for his younger self.

Not because it would have made everything perfect.

But because it would have prevented the avoidable damage. The kind that comes from forgetting, for a moment, that other people get turns.

These five questions are not clever. They are not trendy. They will not impress anyone in the room.

They will, however, save you from explaining later why something "made scnse at the time."

Question 1

Who reacts first, and how uncomfortable does that make them?

Not who you hope reacts.

Who can't afford not to.

Competitors with fragile positioning react quickly.

Partners with thin margins react defensively.

Customers with alternatives react opportunistically.

If your plan assumes the most threatened player stays calm, pause.

Game theory's blunt advice:

The most uncomfortable player moves first.

Question 2

What behavior are we training if this works?

This is the question most launches skip entirely.

If this succeeds:

- Do customers learn to wait?

- Do competitors learn to copy?

- Do sales teams learn to push harder?

- Do partners learn to renegotiate?

Short-term wins are teachers. They teach habits.

If you don't like the habit you're creating, you don't like the strategy. You just like the applause.

Question 3

What does this signal that we didn't mean to say?

You know what you meant.

The market will infer what fits its existing beliefs.

Price changes signal confidence or desperation.

Speed signals control or panic.

Silence signals strength or confusion.

If two interpretations exist, assume the least flattering one spreads faster.

Game theory doesn't assume goodwill. It assumes inference.

Question 4

What happens the second time we do this?

One-off moves are easy to justify. Repeated moves define you.

The second time is when:

- Expectations lock in

- Reputation updates

- Equilibrium shifts

If this move becomes a pattern, are you still comfortable?

If not, it's not a tactic. It's a trap.

Question 5

Who inside the organization is this rewarding by accident?

This one separates strategy from theater.

Does this reward:

- Speed over judgment?
- Volume over value?
- Noise over learning?
- Short-term metrics over long-term trust?

If internal incentives pull against the intent, the incentives win.

They always do.

The Whiteboard Check

When I write these five questions on the whiteboard, nobody argues.

They sigh.

Because the answers are usually obvious. What's hard is acting on them when the calendar, the budget, and the dashboard are shouting.

Game theory doesn't remove pressure. It clarifies it.

The Graybeard Rule About Discipline

Here's the quiet truth:

Most strategy failures are not due to lack of insight.

They're due to lack of follow-through when pressure arrives.

These questions don't make you bold.

They make you deliberate.

And deliberation, in a reactive world, is rare enough to be an advantage.

Where We End

This book didn't try to turn you into a theorist.

It tried to remind you of something you already knew but kept setting aside:

- Other people think
- They remember
- They respond
- And they adapt

Game theory is not a trick for winning.

It's a lens for seeing the game you're already playing clearly enough to stop being surprised by the outcomes.

Which is the real payoff.

Marker capped.

Whiteboard full.

Game still on.

Just played better now.

Chapter Seventeen

Why Marketing Departments Keep Playing the Wrong Game

Every few years, someone declares that marketing is broken.

Too tactical.

Too fluffy.

Too obsessed with clicks.

Too disconnected from revenue.

Game theory listens patiently and replies:

You're not broken. You're just playing several different games at once and pretending they're the same one.

The Department That Can't Agree on the Win Condition

Inside most marketing departments, three games are happening simultaneously:

1. The Visibility Game

> Awareness. Reach. Engagement. Applause.

2. The Performance Game

> Leads. Conversions. Cost per acquisition. Dashboards.

3. The Strategy Game

> Positioning. Differentiation. Long-term advantage.

Each game has different rules. Different incentives. Different timelines.

And they are rarely aligned.

Game theory calls this misaligned objectives. Marketers call it "internal tension."

The Whiteboard Truth Nobody Likes

On the whiteboard, I draw three columns:

What we're rewarded for

What leadership says they want

What actually helps long-term strategy

The overlaps are usually… aspirational.

When people are evaluated on short-term metrics, they rationally optimize short-term outcomes. When strategy asks for patience, it often gets applause instead of protection.

This is not hypocrisy. It's incentives doing their job.

Why Marketing Ends Up Tactical by Default

Strategy requires restraint.

Tactics reward motion.

Marketing is one of the few functions where doing more feels like progress, even when it isn't.

Launch something.

Post something.

Test something.

Optimize something.

Game theory predicts this drift. When activity is visible and outcomes are delayed, action wins over deliberation.

The result is motion without direction.

The Tragedy of the "Center of Excellence"

Many organizations respond by creating centers of excellence, frameworks, and governance.

On paper, this should help.

In practice, it often creates a new game:

- Who controls the narrative
- Who owns the budget
- Who approves the work
- Who gets blamed when results lag

Game theory again: when authority is unclear, politics fill the gap.

Strategy doesn't fail loudly. It suffocates quietly.

Why Marketing Is Asked to Do the Impossible

Marketing is often expected to:

- Drive growth
- Protect the brand
- React instantly
- Plan long-term
- Be creative
- Be predictable

These goals are not compatible without explicit trade-offs.

Game theory demands you choose which game matters most at any given moment. Marketing is rarely allowed that clarity.

So it hedges. And hedging looks like confusion.

The Graybeard Rule About Playing the Right Game

Here it is:

If you don't explicitly choose the game, the loudest incentive will choose it for you.

And the loudest incentive is almost always short-term visibility.

What Needs to Change

This is not a call for more frameworks.

It's a call for:

- Clear priorities
- Protected time horizons
- Metrics that don't sabotage meaning
- Leadership willing to tolerate quiet periods

Game theory doesn't promise comfort. It promises coherence.

Setting Up the Final Turn

We've now looked at:

- Markets
- Competitors
- Customers
- Incentives
- Structures
- Internal politics

There's only one thing left.

What does a strategist actually do, day to day, to keep all of this from slipping away the moment the next urgent request arrives?

That's where we end.

Not with a theory.

With a practice.

Marker down.

One last class..

CHAPTER EIGHTEEN
Thinking One Move Further Than Everyone Else

By the time you reach this chapter, the big reveal should feel… underwhelming.

No secret formula.

No master framework.

No triumphant "aha" moment with fireworks.

Just a quiet advantage.

Thinking one move further than the room.

That's it. That's the whole trick.

Why One Move Is Enough

Movies teach us that great strategists see ten moves ahead.

Game theory sighs and says, "Unnecessary."

Most competitors struggle to see past their current incentives. Most organizations are trapped in the next meeting, the next quarter, the next metric refresh.

If you can reliably think one move further:

- What happens after this works?
- What happens after it fails?
- What happens when others adapt?

You're already ahead.

Not because you're smarter. Because you're patient.

The Whiteboard Habit That Changes Everything

The most valuable strategic tool is not a framework.

It's a pause.

Before approving anything, get to a whiteboard and ask three questions:

1. What are we doing?

2. What do others do next?

3. What do we do then?

That third question is where strategy begins.

Most plans never reach it.

Why Surprise Is Not the Goal

A common misunderstanding:

"If we surprise them, we win."

Surprise is fleeting. Adaptation is inevitable.

Game theory teaches that the goal is not surprise. It's shaping expectations.

When others expect you to:

- Hold your position
- Act consistently
- Respond proportionately
- Play the long game

They behave differently around you.

That's power.

The Calm Advantage

The best strategists look boring.

They don't chase.

They don't overreact.

They don't announce every move.

They let others burn energy while they preserve options.

Game theory explains this calm. When you've already thought through the next move, urgency loses its grip.

The Graybeard Rule to End On

Write this one where you'll see it often:

Strategy is not about outthinking everyone.

It's about outlasting bad incentives and short memories.

Most mistakes happen not from ignorance, but from pressure.

Thinking one move further is how you resist it.

Closing the Whiteboard

If this book has done its job, you won't walk away quoting game theory.

You'll walk away asking better questions:

- Who reacts?
- What does this teach?
- What happens next?
- What are we locking in?
- What game are we actually playing?

Those questions won't make meetings shorter.

They will make outcomes better.

The marker is capped now.

The board is full.

The game continues.

Just with fewer surprises.

When the Marker Runs Dry

At some point, every whiteboard marker gives up.

It doesn't announce it. It fades. The line gets thinner. You press harder. The squeak turns into a rasp. And eventually you're standing there, drawing nothing, pretending the room can still see your point.

That's about right.

Because strategy doesn't end with a conclusion. It ends with maintenance.

The game doesn't stop.

The market doesn't freeze.

Competitors don't retire out of courtesy.

What changes, if you're paying attention, is how often you're surprised.

Early in your career, surprises feel exciting. Later, they feel expensive.

Game theory doesn't remove uncertainty. It removes denial.

It reminds you that:

- Other people notice

- They remember

- They respond

- And they adapt faster than your deck does

Once you accept that, strategy stops being a performance and starts being a discipline.

You stop asking, "Is this clever?"

You start asking, "What does this teach?"

You stop chasing novelty.

You start respecting consistency.

You stop assuming goodwill.

You start designing for incentives.

That's the graybeard shift.

Not cynicism.

Clarity.

The whiteboard stays. The marker gets replaced. The questions remain the same.

Who reacts?

What happens next?

What game are we shaping?

If you keep asking those, you won't win every round.

But you'll stop losing for reasons that should have been obvious.

And in markets like these, that's not a small thing.

Now go clean the board.

Someone else is about to walk in and start explaining how the market works.

You already know better.

Acknowledgments

This book exists because a lot of people were patient while I learned things the slow way.

First, thank you to the students. The ones who asked the uncomfortable questions. The ones who challenged tidy answers. The ones who stared at the whiteboard long enough to realize it wasn't trying to impress them, it was trying to tell the truth. Every good idea in this book was sharpened by a raised eyebrow in the back of the room.

To the colleagues and collaborators who trusted me with real problems instead of hypotheticals. Thank you for letting me see what happens when incentives collide, when dashboards lie politely, and when smart people are rewarded for doing the wrong thing very efficiently. You taught me more than any case study ever could.

To the marketers, strategists, and leaders who shared stories that started with "this seemed like a good idea at the time." Those stories are the backbone of this book. You know who you are. I didn't name names on purpose.

To the competitors who reacted exactly the way game theory said they would. You were excellent teachers, whether you meant to be or not.

To the mentors who taught me restraint. Who reminded me that clever fades faster than consistent, and that thinking one move further beats thinking ten moves loudly. Your influence is all over these pages, even when the jokes are mine.

To the organizations that tolerated whiteboards over slide decks, pauses over urgency, and questions that slowed meetings down before they sped outcomes up. Thank you for understanding that clarity is not inefficiency.

To my family, who lived with someone who couldn't stop explaining why people behaved the way they did at restaurants, in airports, and during commercials.

And finally, to the marker. The squeaky one. The half-dried one. The one that refused to glide smoothly and forced ideas to earn their place on the board. You were right more often than the slides ever were.

Glossary of Terms

Action

What a player actually does, not what they say they will do. Markets respond to actions. Decks do not.

Adaptation

The process by which customers, competitors, or partners change behavior after learning from your last move. This is why launches don't freeze reality.

Asymmetric Information

A situation where one party knows something the other doesn't. Marketing is mostly about managing what people think you know.

Best Practice

A stable pattern of behavior adopted by many players, often because no one wants to risk being first to stop doing it.

Bounded Rationality

The idea that people try to be rational, but within limits of time, information, and attention. This explains most "irrational" behavior.

Credibility

The market's belief that you will do what you say you'll do, even when it's inconvenient. Hard to build. Easy to spend.

Cooperation

Mutually beneficial behavior that persists because retaliation is possible and memory exists.

Defection

Choosing short-term advantage over cooperation. Often rational once. Dangerous when repeated.

Dominant Strategy

An action that performs better regardless of what others do. Rare in real markets. Overused in pitch decks.

Engagement

Observable activity that feels meaningful but does not necessarily indicate understanding, commitment, or value.

Equilibrium

A stable state where no player can improve outcomes by changing behavior alone. Often mistaken for "the way things have to be."

External Games

Strategic interactions with customers, competitors, partners, or markets where outcomes depend on others' responses.

First-Mover Advantage

The benefit of acting early when it creates lasting structural advantage. Not guaranteed. Often romanticized.

Folk Theorem

A game theory result showing that many outcomes are possible in repeated games, depending on incentives and punishment. Translation: behavior matters more than rules.

Game

Any situation where outcomes depend on the choices of more than one decision-maker. If other people get turns, you're in one.

Incentives

What the system rewards, explicitly or implicitly. Incentives win arguments without raising their voice.

Information Signal

An action taken to convey meaning when words aren't trusted. Prices, speed, silence, and consistency all signal.

Internal Game

The strategic interactions inside an organization shaped by incentives, metrics, and politics, often more influential than the external market.

Local Optima

A situation where each part of the organization improves its own results while the whole gets worse.

Loyalty

Repeat behavior driven by expectation, habit, or trust. Not the same as affection.

Market Memory

The accumulation of past behavior that shapes expectations. Markets forget slowly and selectively.

Misaligned Objectives

When different teams are rewarded for different outcomes, causing rational behavior that undermines overall strategy.

Nash Equilibrium

A situation where no player can do better by changing strategy alone. Stable, not necessarily good.

Payoff

The result a player receives from an interaction. Not always financial. Reputation counts.

Pattern Breaking

Deliberately changing behavior to escape equilibrium without triggering destructive retaliation.

Platform

A structure that enables and constrains behavior by others. Platforms design games rather than play them.

Punishment

A response intended to deter future defection. Must be credible, proportional, and survivable.

Rational Behavior

Behavior that makes sense given incentives and information. Predictable does not mean optimal.

Reputation

Shared belief about how a player behaves over time. Memory at scale.

Repeated Game

A game played multiple times where past behavior affects future outcomes. Most business fits here.

Retaliation

A response to defection meant to change expectations. Overuse teaches the wrong lesson.

Second Move

What happens after your initial action succeeds or fails. Where strategy actually begins.

Signal Jamming

When too many actions contradict each other, making intentions unclear. Common in reactive organizations.

Stalemate

An equilibrium where no one improves outcomes because deviation feels risky. Often mislabeled as stability.

Trust

The expectation that another party will behave predictably and fairly over time. Built slowly. Broken quickly.

Unintended Consequences

Outcomes that arise because others adapt to incentives you didn't notice you created.

Win-Win

An outcome where all parties benefit and expect the behavior to continue. Rare without structure.

Bibliography

Foundational Game Theory *(Books)*

Axelrod, R. (1984). The evolution of cooperation. Basic Books.

Dixit, A. K., & Nalebuff, B. J. (2008). The art of strategy: A game theorist's guide to success in business and life. W. W. Norton & Company.

Fudenberg, D., & Tirole, J. (1991). Game theory. MIT Press.

Gibbons, R. (1992). Game theory for applied economists. Princeton University Press.

Luce, R. D., & Raiffa, H. (1957). Games and decisions: Introduction and critical survey. John Wiley & Sons.

Osborne, M. J. (2004). An introduction to game theory. Oxford University Press.

Osborne, M. J., & Rubinstein, A. (1994). A course in game theory. MIT Press.

Schelling, T. C. (1960). The strategy of conflict. Harvard University Press.

Schelling, T. C. (1978). Micromotives and macrobehavior. W. W. Norton & Company.

von Neumann, J., & Morgenstern, O. (1944). Theory of games and economic behavior. Princeton University Press.

Peer-Reviewed Journal Articles: Game Theory & Strategic Interaction

Aumann, R. J. (1999). Interactive epistemology I: Knowledge. International Journal of Game Theory, 28(3), 263–300. https://doi.org/10.1007/s001820050111

Fudenberg, D., & Maskin, E. (1986). The folk theorem in repeated games with discounting or with incomplete information. Econometrica, 54(3), 533–554. https://doi.org/10.2307/1911307

Kreps, D. M., Milgrom, P., Roberts, J., & Wilson, R. (1982). Rational cooperation in the finitely repeated prisoners' dilemma. Journal of Economic Theory, 27(2), 245–252. https://doi.org/10.1016/0022-0531(82)90029-1

Mailath, G. J., & Samuelson, L. (2001). Who wants a good reputation? Review of Economic Studies, 68(2), 415–441. https://doi.org/10.1111/1467-937X.00175

Selten, R. (1975). Reexamination of the perfectness concept for equilibrium points in extensive games. International Journal of Game Theory, 4(1), 25–55. https://doi.org/10.1007/BF01766400

Strategy, Competition, and Market Behavior

Brandenburger, A. M., & Stuart, H. W. (1996). Value-based business strategy. Journal of Economics & Management Strategy, 5(1), 5–24. https://doi.org/10.1111/j.1430-9134.1996.00005.x

Porter, M. E. (1980). Competitive strategy: Techniques for analyzing industries and competitors. Academy of Management Review, 5(1), 103–107. https://doi.org/10.5465/amr.1980.4288962

Rumelt, R. P., Schendel, D., & Teece, D. J. (1991). Strategic management and economics. Strategic Management Journal, 12(S2), 5–29. https://doi.org/10.1002/smj.4250121003

Organizational Behavior, Incentives, and Internal Games

Holmström, B. (1979). Moral hazard and observability. Bell Journal of Economics, 10(1), 74–91. https://doi.org/10.2307/3003320

Kerr, S. (1975). On the folly of rewarding A while hoping for B. Academy of Management Journal, 18(4), 769–783. https://doi.org/10.2307/255378

March, J. G. (1991). Exploration and exploitation in organizational learning. Organization Science, 2(1), 71–87. https://doi.org/10.1287/orsc.2.1.71

Williamson, O. E. (1979). Transaction-cost economics: The governance of contractual relations. Journal of Law and Economics, 22(2), 233–261. https://doi.org/10.1086/466942

While this book avoids formal proofs and notation, it is grounded in decades of peer-reviewed research in game theory, behavioral economics, and organizational behavior.

The selected articles support the central claim that strategic outcomes emerge not from isolated decisions, but from repeated interaction, incentives, and mutual belief formation.

.

About the Author

Mark "Dr. Maddog" Donnelly, PhD, is the graybeard lecturer who turned a squeaky whiteboard and tweed sportcoat into a teaching philosophy. A marketing professor, brand consultant, author of 50+ books, historian, photographer, and creative instigator, he's spent decades making complex ideas feel simple – and making students wonder if it's all that coffee he drinks, or is he naturally this intense.

Dr. Donnelly built his reputation the old-fashioned way: by simplifying the truth. Not the buzzword-stuffed, corporate-approved version, but the real, human kind you only learn after watching trends rise, fall, and come back wearing different shoes.

Along with over 30 years in academia, he's wandered through newspapers, publishing, consulting, community work, and philanthropic strategy - collecting stories, experience, and more old books than any one man needs. Today, his whiteboard scribbles still inspire everyone from Master classes to CEOs, finally captured in print before the janitor could erase them.

Ask him what he truly is and he'll shrug:
"A teacher at heart.
A storyteller by accident.
A graybeard by mileage."

He lives and creates in Buffalo, New York, with his bride Princess Laura and an ever-expanding pile of notebooks and half-finished ideas. His lifelong guiding principle remains simple:

Make a difference.

This book is his latest attempt to do exactly that.

Other Timeless Books in the Graybeard Lectures Series:

Each stands alone.
Together, they form a unique, common sense curriculum.

Graybeard Lectures: Marketing

Drawn from smudged whiteboards and lived experience, This book cuts through buzzwords and trends to reveal how branding, storytelling, word of mouth, and purpose actually work—by understanding humans first. Warm, humorous, and practical, it's a guide for anyone who wants marketing that makes sense and lasts.

Graybeard Lectures: Advertising

Advertising doesn't fail because people stopped paying attention. It fails because it forgets how attention works.

This book explores why the most effective advertising aligns with human instincts rather than fighting them. It examines timing, context, repetition, and emotional truth without chasing trends or tactics.

Graybeard Lectures: Market Research

Listening Past The Numbers is a clear-eyed look at why market research often delivers confidence instead of understanding. It challenges the misuse of data, dashboards, and statistics, arguing for research grounded in human behavior, context, and judgment. Rather than offering tools, the book offers a wiser way to think, listen, and decide when the numbers start acting certain.

Graybeard Lectures: Branding

Branding is not decoration. It's definition.This book challenges the modern habit of treating brands as visual projects instead of behavioral ones. Logos matter less than promises kept. Consistency matters more than cleverness. Reputation is built slowly and lost quickly.